DK Pocket Eyewitness

CARS

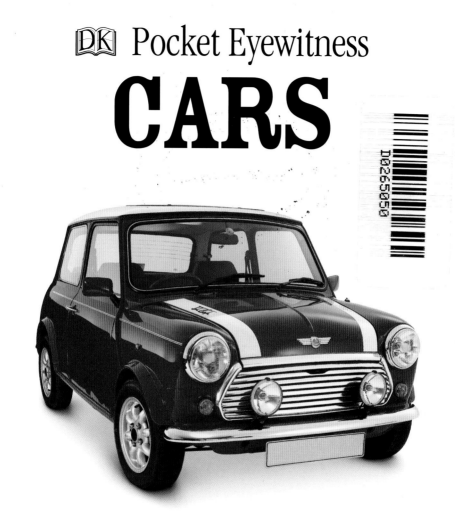

FACTS AT YOUR FINGERTIPS

Penguin
Random
House

DK DELHI
Project editor Bharti Bedi
Editor Suneha Dutta
Assistant editor Sonam Mathur
Project art editor Nishesh Batnagar
Art editor Amit Varma
DTP designer Jaypal Singh
Picture researcher Sakshi Saluja
Jacket designer Dhirendra Singh
Managing editor Alka Thakur Hazarika
Managing art editor Romi Chakraborty
Pre-production manager Balwant Singh
Production manager Pankaj Sharma

DK UK
Senior editor Caroline Stamps
Senior art editor Spencer Holbrook
Managing editor Gareth Jones
Managing art editor Philip Letsu
Jacket editor Claire Gell
Jacket designer Laura Brim
Jacket design development manager
Sophia M. Tampakopoulos Turner
Producer (pre-production) Adam Stoneham
Producer (print production) Vivienne Yong

Publisher Andrew Macintyre
Associate publishing director Liz Wheeler
Art director Phil Ormerod
Publishing director Jonathan Metcalf

Consultant Giles Chapman

First published in Great Britain in 2016
by Dorling Kindersley Limited
80 Strand, London WC2R 0RL

Copyright © 2016 Dorling Kindersley Limited
A Penguin Random House Company

10 9 8 7 6 5 4 3 2 1
001–187505–March/16

A CIP catalogue record for this book
is available from the British Library.

ISBN: 978-1-4093-4785-9

Printed and bound by South China
Printing Company, China

Discover more at
www.dk.com

CONTENTS

Scales and sizes
The *Cars in space* section of this book contains scale drawings of space rovers against a human body to show their size.

1.8 m (6 ft)

1931 La Salle

What is a car?

A car is a vehicle that is specifically designed to carry people. Its basic structure is made up of a steel frame called a chassis. A typical car has four wheels and is powered by an engine, which uses fuel of some kind.

Steering wheel moves the wheels to change the car's direction

Wiper cleans dirt off the windscreen and gives the driver a clear view of the road ahead

Dashboard features controls and instruments, such as the speedometer and the fuel gauge

Bonnet covers the engine

Battery powers electrical systems, such as lights and ignition

Grille allows air into the radiator, helping to keep the engine cool

Engine powers the car's movement

On the inside

All the functions of a car are controlled from the interior with the help of a steering wheel, gear stick, and foot pedals. The seats are padded for comfort.

Headlight lights the road at night

Wing (fender) stops spray and grit flying off the tyres

Antenna receives signals for the in-car radio

Boot can be used to store luggage

Window pillar gives strength to the car's frame

Window allows nearly all-round vision from interior

Rear light indicates whether the car is braking

Bumper acts as a cushion against impacts

Axle (metal bar) connects the wheels

Wheel turns on an axle

Door gives the driver and any passengers access to interior

Door mirror lets the driver see rear and side

HOT AND COLD

Numerous tests are carried out on a new car model to make sure that all parts perform as expected in extreme weather conditions. This car is being tested to check if all its parts work efficiently in freezing conditions.

History of the car

Cars have come a long way since the first self-propelled vehicle hit the road in 1769. Over the years, numerous inventions and technological developments have helped to shape the cars that we drive today.

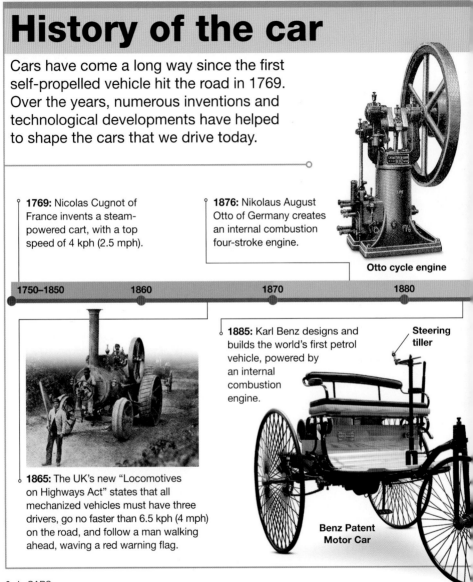

1769: Nicolas Cugnot of France invents a steam-powered cart, with a top speed of 4 kph (2.5 mph).

1876: Nikolaus August Otto of Germany creates an internal combustion four-stroke engine.

Otto cycle engine

1750–1850   1860   1870   1880

1885: Karl Benz designs and builds the world's first petrol vehicle, powered by an internal combustion engine.

Steering tiller

1865: The UK's new "Locomotives on Highways Act" states that all mechanized vehicles must have three drivers, go no faster than 6.5 kph (4 mph) on the road, and follow a man walking ahead, waving a red warning flag.

Benz Patent Motor Car

Motorized carriage

1886: Gottlieb Daimler of Germany fits a petrol engine to a horseless carriage, creating the world's first four-wheeled petrol car. It reaches 16 kph (10 mph).

1890   1900

1889: In France, René Panhard and Émile Levassor become the world's first car manufacturers, building motor vehicles for sale.

1891: René Panhard builds the first car with an engine at the front.

Panhard's Phaeton

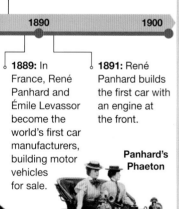

GAME CHANGERS

Certain cars changed the history of the car industry. Hugely popular in their day, these cars are now prized classics.

BENZ VELO
Before 1894, each new car was unique. The first car built to a standard design was the Benz Velo – 134 identical Velos were produced.

MERCEDES-BENZ 260D
The first diesel passenger car – the Mercedes-Benz 260D – arrived in 1936. By 1939, there was a 15-month waiting list for the car.

THE BEETLE
Volkswagen started the mass-market production of the Type 38 (later called the Beetle) in Germany, in 1938.

FERRARI 125 SPORT
In 1947, the Ferrari 125 Sport was launched – the first car under the Ferrari brand name.

THE AUSTIN MINI
An affordable small car, the Austin Mini had a spacious interior. It was launched as an alternative to the slow and unsafe microcars (very small cars) of the 1950s.

1923: Alfred Sloan, president of General Motors, introduces the idea of changing a car's style every year.

1900: Wilhelm Maybach creates the Mercedes 35 hp racing car, with a top speed of 86 kph (53 mph).

1900	1910	1920	1930	1940	1950

1901: The two-seater Oldsmobile Curved Dash arrives. It is the USA's first mass-produced petrol-powered car, with 425 cars built in its first year.

1908: The iconic Ford Model T is launched. It is the first low-priced mass-produced car, built using inexpensive raw materials.

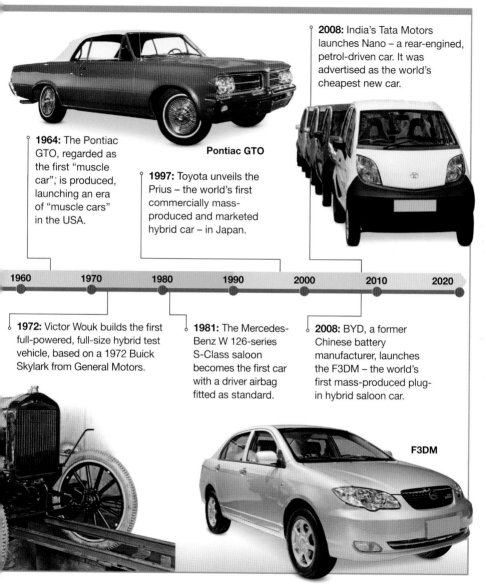

2008: India's Tata Motors launches Nano – a rear-engined, petrol-driven car. It was advertised as the world's cheapest new car.

1964: The Pontiac GTO, regarded as the first "muscle car", is produced, launching an era of "muscle cars" in the USA.

Pontiac GTO

1997: Toyota unveils the Prius – the world's first commercially mass-produced and marketed hybrid car – in Japan.

1960	1970	1980	1990	2000	2010	2020

1972: Victor Wouk builds the first full-powered, full-size hybrid test vehicle, based on a 1972 Buick Skylark from General Motors.

1981: The Mercedes-Benz W 126-series S-Class saloon becomes the first car with a driver airbag fitted as standard.

2008: BYD, a former Chinese battery manufacturer, launches the F3DM – the world's first mass-produced plug-in hybrid saloon car.

F3DM

How an engine works

Most cars today are powered by an internal combustion engine. This is so-called because inside ("internal") the engine, small explosions ("combustion") make pistons move. This moves other parts to turn the car's wheels.

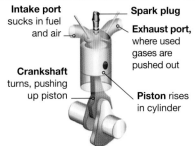

Intake port sucks in fuel and air

Spark plug

Exhaust port, where used gases are pushed out

Crankshaft turns, pushing up piston

Piston rises in cylinder

Engine cylinders

Internal combustion engines contain cylinders. When the engine fires, a rod called the crankshaft pushes a piston up into each cylinder, squeezing a fuel-air mixture. A tiny explosion results, pushing the piston down again. This is repeated along all the cylinders, keeping the crankshaft turning.

From engine to wheels

The crankshaft collects power from the cylinders and transfers it to the wheels via the gearbox. In a front-wheel drive car, as shown here, the gears inside the gearbox turn to pass on the power to two places – the front axle, which controls the front wheels, and the drive shaft, which works the rear axle and the rear wheels.

TYPES OF ENGINE

Internal combustion engine designs vary in the number of cylinders they have, and how they are arranged.

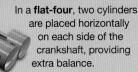

In a **flat-four**, two cylinders are placed horizontally on each side of the crankshaft, providing extra balance.

A **straight-four**, or inline, is the most common layout. It has an upright, or slanting, row of four cylinders and makes efficient use of fuel.

In a **V6 engine**, two rows of three cylinders are arranged in a "V". It is good for high-performance and racing cars.

Front and rear axles (rod-like parts) transmit power to the wheels

In **front-wheel drive** (where only the front wheels are powered), the engine is always in the front

Gears alter the engine's power so the wheels turn at the speed the driver needs

The **drive shaft** carries power to the rear wheels

Inside a factory

Car production is a complex process. Cars are built on an assembly line, where the procedure is split into many stages, involving robots as well as humans. Several quality checks and tests are carried out before the cars are finally transported to the showroom.

Freshly painted

After the car's body is put together, it is prepared for painting. Robots spray several layers of paint onto it. After the final coat, the car is placed on a conveyer that takes it to be "baked" at high temperatures, which makes the paint more durable.

Making the car body

Metal sheets (usually steel or aluminium) are cut and moulded to form the body panels and roof of each car. These are welded onto the car's frame by robots. Each car is then given its own vehicle identification number (VIN).

Finishing the job

After being painted, cars are moved along the assembly line to be fitted with parts. The engine and gearbox are pushed into place from underneath. Robots then fix the doors and wheels to the chassis. At this stage, all other components of the car, such as the steering wheel and electrical systems, are fixed to their respective places.

Ready to go

The cars then go through various tests to check that all the different components – such as the brakes, engine, and steering wheel – are functioning properly. Finally, each car is cleared to be sent to the showroom.

New car, old car

Around 60 million cars are produced each year. After leaving the factory, the cars are transported to showrooms where they are put on sale, or exported for sale in other countries. A car owner may resell his vehicle, or send it to a scrapyard if it is beyond repair. At the scrapyard, different parts of the car are recycled to be used again.

Cars can be driven on and off a **car carrier**

Leaving the factory

New cars are delivered locally by train or in car transporters. They are also exported on ships called car carriers. A large car carrier can hold 8,000 cars. The biggest car carrier, the *Triple-E*, can carry 36,000 cars!

Each car has a **protective cover** while being transported

Goodbye, car!

Few cars end up in landfill. Most go to a scrapyard to be stripped for spare parts that can be used to repair other cars. Fluids, such as oil and antifreeze, are sent for recycling, along with the tyres and metal body parts.

Crushed cars

Crush that car!

The remains of old or smashed cars are often squashed. They are then easier to transport to a recycling plant for melting down.

Most countries have recycling laws. About 80 per cent of a car can be recycled.

A car's engine may be reconditioned (restored) or the metal may be recycled.

The chassis (base) of a car is usually melted down for the metal it contains.

The **heavy metals** and chemicals in car batteries can also be reused.

Safety measures

New cars undergo a lot of tests to make sure they are safe to drive. One of the most valuable of these tests is the use of crash test dummies – life-sized models of people. The results from these tests are recorded and analysed to improve a car's design as well as safety features, such as airbags and seat belts.

An adult **dummy** usually weighs up to 77 kg (170 lb) and is 1.8 m (6 ft) tall

Smart dummies

More than 130 sensors are fitted to each crash test dummy. During safety tests, these sensors record all sorts of important data.

Crumple zone absorbs some of the impact in head-on collisions

Airbag inflates to cushion the impact if a crash occurs

Track testing

Various track tests study how a new car will perform on the road. For example, a "moose" test studies how well a car can swerve to avoid obstacles that may suddenly appear.

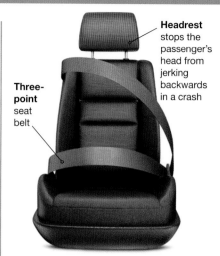

Headrest stops the passenger's head from jerking backwards in a crash

Three-point seat belt

Safety belt

Seat belts ensure that a car's passengers do not fall out of their seats in the event of a crash. It is the law to wear a seat belt in most countries.

What if it crashes?

Modern cars are built to absorb the impact of a crash. For this, each end of the car has a crumple zone – an area designed to crush and crumple on collision. Airbags are additional safety features, which quickly inflate to cushion the front seat occupants in the event of a crash.

Tyre needs good tread (grip) and correct air pressure to steer and brake efficiently

Engineers use mist or smoke illuminated by

lasers

to study the way air flows around a car in a wind tunnel

WIND TUNNEL TESTING

A wind tunnel is a huge, tube-like structure with huge electric fans at one end that create high speed winds. A car undergoing the test is parked inside this tunnel. Different instruments help to study the airflow around the car and test how aerodynamic it is. Cutting through the air accounts for around 15 per cent of a car's fuel use, so wind tunnel testing is important to a car's designers.

Early cars

The earliest cars were steam-powered. They were usually simple carriages fitted with an engine, as car makers were heavily influenced by the design of horse-drawn carriages. Inventors then tried to build cars suitable for everyday use, which led to the appearance of engines powered by petrol and electricity. Many other innovations, such as the windscreen wiper and steering wheel, followed.

FUEL METER
In 1914, car manufacturer Studebaker installed the first dash-mounted petrol gauge, showing how much fuel was in the car. These became a standard feature in the 1920s.

Cars from the past

Early powered vehicles were "horseless carts" driven by steam, and the first designs were inspired by carriages. The late 19th century saw several technological developments, but the age of cars truly began in 1908 with Henry Ford's moving assembly line for his Model T.

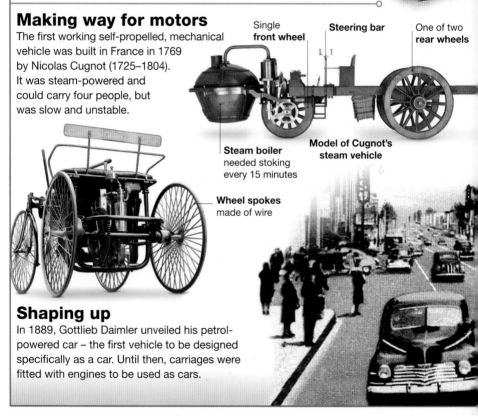

Making way for motors

The first working self-propelled, mechanical vehicle was built in France in 1769 by Nicolas Cugnot (1725–1804). It was steam-powered and could carry four people, but was slow and unstable.

Single **front wheel**

Steering bar

One of two **rear wheels**

Steam boiler needed stoking every 15 minutes

Model of Cugnot's steam vehicle

Wheel spokes made of wire

Shaping up

In 1889, Gottlieb Daimler unveiled his petrol-powered car – the first vehicle to be designed specifically as a car. Until then, carriages were fitted with engines to be used as cars.

Model T

Henry Ford's moving assembly line revolutionized car manufacturing by making the mass production of vehicles faster and more organized. The Ford Motor Company sold more than 15 million Model T cars between 1908 and 1927.

Changing face

The 1920s were a golden age for the car industry as cars became smaller and more affordable and reliable, attracting more buyers. Sports cars, such as this 1927 OM 665 Superba, were also developed for leisure use and racing.

After the war

By the 1950s, the market for cars had grown as companies began to sell their models to international markets as well. Many American families owned a car and the roads became busier.

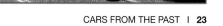

Before 1920

Building the first cars was a remarkable feat. However, manufacturing them in large numbers and convincing the public to buy these new types of vehicle proved to be hard. Until about 1920, the USA was producing the most cars, followed by France, the UK, and Germany.

Peugeot Type 5

The Type 5 was the second petrol car model that Peugeot came out with after the Type 2. It had face-to-face seating. In 1894, this car took part in the world's first motor car competition.

YEAR	1894
ORIGIN	France
ENGINE	565 cc, twin-cylinder

TOP SPEED
18 kph
(11 mph)

Arrol-Johnston 10 HP Dogcart

Developed by George Johnston in Glasgow, Scotland, the Dogcart was the first car to be built in the UK, remaining in production for a decade. The model was designed with its engine placed below the floor of the car.

YEAR	1897
ORIGIN	UK
ENGINE	3,230 cc, flat-two

TOP SPEED
40 kph (25 mph)

Mercedes 60 hp

One of the most advanced cars of its time in terms of engineering and design, the Mercedes 60 hp was among the fastest cars in the early 1900s. Its design was aimed at improving passenger comfort.

YEAR 1903
ORIGIN Germany
ENGINE 9,236 cc, straight-four
TOP SPEED 117 kph (73 mph)

Bonnet

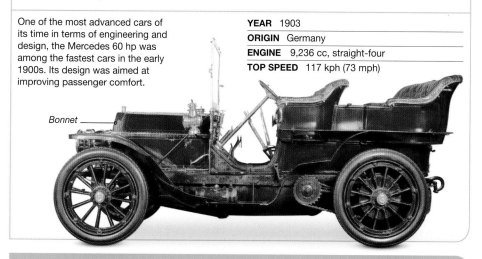

Rolls-Royce Silver Ghost 40/50 hp

At first, only one car in the 40/50 hp series was called Silver Ghost. Later, all cars of this model were given this name. It became well known as a reliable car, and was produced until 1925.

YEAR 1906
ORIGIN UK
ENGINE 7,036 cc, straight-six
TOP SPEED 121 kph (75 mph)

1920–1935

As affordable car models became available in the 1920s, the demand for cars gradually grew. Sports and racing cars also gained popularity. By the 1930s, smaller, more aerodynamic, and more technologically advanced cars were being produced.

FOCUS ON...
SERVICES

The increase in the sale of cars led to growth in other businesses, such as petrol stations, repair shops, and motels.

▲ Before the first petrol station was built in 1905 in Missouri, USA, petrol was sold at pharmacies.

▲ As long-distance travel became common, motor hotels – or motels – began to appear along major American roads, providing cheap accommodation for motorists.

▲ Other roadside businesses, such as diners and similar places to eat, also thrived.

Bugatti Type 35B

The Type 35 was a successful racing car and could also be driven on roads. A member of the Type 35 family, the Type 35B was the last version to be produced in the series.

YEAR	1927
ORIGIN	France
ENGINE	2,262 cc, straight-eight
TOP SPEED	204 kph (127 mph)

Mudguard for use on road

Small windscreen to shield driver from wind

Eight-spoke, cast-aluminium wheel

Duesenberg Model J

The fastest and most powerful car in the American market at the time it was produced, the Model J was designed to appeal to the rich and famous. It was also launched in Europe, where it proved a worthy competitor to the big, luxurious cars already available there.

YEAR 1928

ORIGIN USA

ENGINE 6,882 cc, straight-eight

TOP SPEED 192 kph (119 mph)

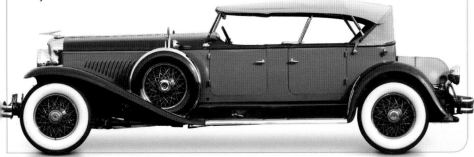

Ford Model Y

Made in the UK for markets outside the USA, the Ford Model Y was seen as Ford's first "foreign" car. It sold well enough to give Ford the leading position among car manufacturers.

YEAR 1932

ORIGIN UK

ENGINE
933 cc,
straight-four

TOP SPEED
92 kph
(57 mph)

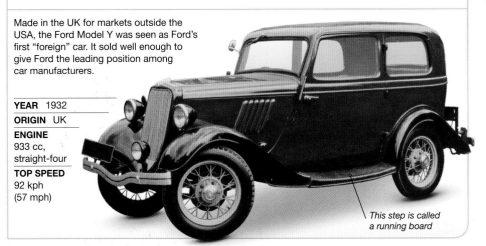

This step is called a running board

Only 14

**egg-shaped, three-wheeler
Brütsch Mopettas
were ever built**

The 1940s and 1950s

During World War II (1939–45), cars were largely produced for military purposes. After the war, affordable and simple family cars were in demand. By the 1950s, however, there was a call for glamour, performance, and style.

Willys MB Jeep

Made for the military, this Jeep was a light, four-wheel drive (where the engine powers all four wheels) utility vehicle for cargo transport and surveillance. It is an iconic World War II car.

YEAR	1941
ORIGIN	USA
ENGINE	2,199 cc, straight-four
TOP SPEED	97 kph (60 mph)

Dodge Coronet

The Dodge Coronet was available in a four-door and a two-door model. This car's clutch was replaced by a fluid-drive transmission, which was operated by a foot pedal. This meant that the driver could stop the car and then start it again in any gear, without using the gear stick or clutch.

YEAR	1949
ORIGIN	USA
ENGINE	3,769 cc, straight-six
TOP SPEED	129 kph (80 mph)

"Whitewall" tyres have a ring of white rubber

Chevrolet Bel Air

Compared to the first Bel Air 1950 model, the 1955 Chevrolet Bel Air boasted a more stylish design, attractive chrome features, and a better engine. The combination made it one of the most desirable cars of its time, and it continues to be prized by collectors.

YEAR	1955
ORIGIN	USA
ENGINE	4,343 cc, V8
TOP SPEED	161 kph (100 mph)

Two-tone paintwork highlights car's sleek appearance

Hooded headlight was a new style feature on this model

Renault Dauphine

After conducting a survey of European drivers in 1951, Renault improved its 4CV economy car and launched the hugely successful Dauphine. This car had a larger engine and more spacious interior than the 4CV. It recorded worldwide sales of two million cars in 12 years.

YEAR	1956
ORIGIN	France
ENGINE	845 cc, straight-four
TOP SPEED	106 kph (66 mph)

The 1960s and 1970s

In the 1960s, cars with simple, almost boxlike, designs became popular. Cars were more compact or more luxurious, while also increasing in their performance and power. In the 1970s, efficiency improved further and safety measures, such as seat belts and airbags, were introduced.

Mini Cooper

The Mini was a small, energy-efficient car that was launched in 1959. In 1961, Formula 1 car designer John Cooper improved its design – adding disc brakes, a powerful motor, and wider wheels – and created the Mini Cooper.

YEAR	1961
ORIGIN	UK
ENGINE	1,275 cc, four-cylinder
TOP SPEED	161 kph (100 mph)

Although only 3 m (10 ft) long, the Mini had enough room inside for a whole family

Jaguar XJ6

Perhaps one of the most significant cars in the company's history, the XJ6 replaced most of Jaguar's saloons. Its design was said to offer a perfect balance of comfort, performance, and power.

YEAR	1968
ORIGIN	UK
ENGINE	4,235 cc, six-cylinder
TOP SPEED	200 kph (124 mph)

Citroën SM

In 1968, Citroën purchased the Italian luxury car manufacturer, Maserati. Their collaboration resulted in the Citroën SM in 1970. This car combined Citroën's aerodynamic design with Maserati's powerful V6 engine.

YEAR	1970
ORIGIN	France
ENGINE	2,670 cc, V6
TOP SPEED	229 kph (142 mph)

Modern cars

From the 1980s, cars were increasingly equipped with new technology, such as parking assistance. Existing features, including the steering wheel and dashboard, were improved. Today, cars are often built with extra features, such as navigation systems and rearview cameras. Engines are more powerful and fuel efficient than in the past, and can handle longer distances.

OFF-ROADING
Sport utility vehicles (SUVs) are designed for "off-roading", where cars are driven on rough terrains, such as in and around forests and over sand.

All shapes and sizes

Buyers choose a car for its features, depending on their requirements. A family may need more seats, a larger boot, and four or even five doors, as opposed to two. Some people may opt for additional features, such as a retracting roof.

Door design

Most car doors are hinged, and can be opened manually or, in heavier models, electronically. Some cars have child-safety locks on their rear doors, so that passengers, especially children, do not accidentally open the doors from inside.

The boot hatch is a fifth door and opens upwards

Roof design

Most cars have a solid roof. They may be fitted with a sunroof (sliding pane). Convertible cars have a retractable roof that folds away or a detachable roof that is taken off.

Boot space

The boot space of an estate car is designed for carrying bulky loads, but even small cars have enough space for carrying shopping bags or luggage.

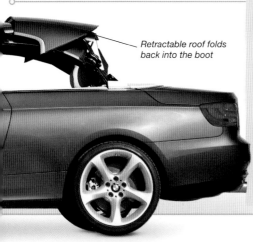

Retractable roof folds back into the boot

The **box design** of a car shows how the car's three main areas – its engine, passenger space, and boot space – are divided into different sections.

In a **one-box** design, the whole interior of the car – including the engine and boot – is designed as one compartment.

A **two-box** design is one in which the engine forms a separate compartment from the passenger and boot space.

A **three-box** design divides the car into three sections – the engine, passenger space, and boot space.

FOCUS ON...
REAR DESIGN

Saloons are grouped according to the shape and slope of the rear section of the car.

▲ In a fastback saloon, the slope stretches from the roof to the base of the boot.

▲ In a notchback saloon, the boot lid and the roof are parallel to the ground. The lid extends back horizontally from the rear windscreen.

▲ In a hatchback saloon, the boot lid covers the entire rear. The rear windscreen lifts up with the lid.

Saloons

Saloon cars have a fixed roof and an enclosed boot, and most models have four doors. Types of saloon include large family cars, compact executives with a smaller rear space, luxury models with powerful engines, and high-performing sports saloons.

Maserati Biturbo

The Maserati brand, known for its high-priced models, wanted to introduce a supercar-style vehicle that was more affordable. The result was the two-door Maserati Biturbo. The car sold well at first, mainly because of its luxurious interior. However, because of technical problems, including engine failures and oil leaks, sales dropped.

YEAR	1981
ORIGIN	Italy
ENGINE	1,996 cc, V6
TOP SPEED	212 kph (132 mph)

The 1984 version of the Maserati Biturbo, with a modified engine, was named the Worst Car of 1984 by *Time* magazine in 2007.

Chrysler LHS

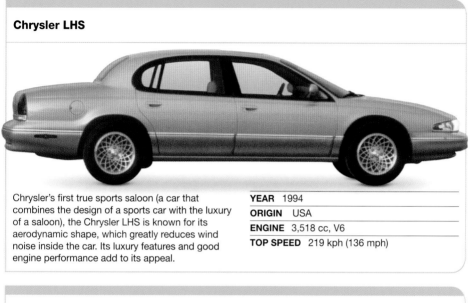

Chrysler's first true sports saloon (a car that combines the design of a sports car with the luxury of a saloon), the Chrysler LHS is known for its aerodynamic shape, which greatly reduces wind noise inside the car. Its luxury features and good engine performance add to its appeal.

YEAR	1994
ORIGIN	USA
ENGINE	3,518 cc, V6
TOP SPEED	219 kph (136 mph)

Bentley Arnage

The sporty, high-end Bentley Arnage was the first car for Bentley Motors to have a completely new design since 1980. Fitted with a special V8 engine, it was a fast and elegant car. The last Bentley Arnage was produced in 2009.

YEAR	1998
ORIGIN	UK
ENGINE	4,398 cc, V8
TOP SPEED	241 kph (150 mph)

Volvo S60

This Volvo was designed to compete with German-made saloons. A number of speed-record attempts and track racing events have shown how powerful the car is. The S60 is even used as a patrol car by some police forces.

YEAR	2000
ORIGIN	Sweden
ENGINE	2,484 cc, straight-five
TOP SPEED	210 kph (130 mph)

Toyota Camry

The Toyota Camry has been one of the best-selling saloons in the USA since 1997. The redesigned model has more room inside, although a smaller boot space, than earlier versions of the car.

YEAR	2007
ORIGIN	Japan
ENGINE	2,362 cc, straight-four
TOP SPEED	210 kph (130 mph)

Toyota has a tradition of using the word "crown" in the names of most of its cars. "Camry" comes from a Japanese word for crown.

BMW 335i

The 335i is extremely powerful. It is the first car in BMW's 3 Series to have a turbocharged petrol engine (extra-powerful yet compact). However, like all German cars, its top speed is artificially limited to 250 kph (155 mph) – high enough for driving on the autobahn (motorways that do not have a speed limit).

YEAR 2007

ORIGIN Germany

ENGINE 2,979 cc, straight-six

TOP SPEED 250 kph (155 mph)

Headlights swivel in the same direction as the steering wheel

Jaguar XJ

Although the Jaguar XJ is a full-sized saloon, its aluminium body makes it lighter than even a standard medium-sized car. Its glass roof extends over the rear seats.

YEAR 2010

ORIGIN UK

ENGINE 5,000 cc, V8

TOP SPEED 250 kph (155 mph)

Sensors on the windscreen automatically activate windscreen wipers when it rains

Toyota Corolla Altis

Toyota made the first Corolla in 1966. The 2011 model is the 12th variation. Like all the Corollas in the past, the Altis' design is focused on reliability over style and technology, though the new engine is smoother and more fuel-efficient.

YEAR 2011

ORIGIN Japan

ENGINE 1,987 cc, straight-four

TOP SPEED 185 kph (115 mph)

Audi A3

The demand for Audi cars in China was one of the factors that led the company to design a saloon version of the A3 series. It has a high-performance engine and a luxury design, but less luggage space than the hatchback version.

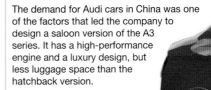

YEAR 2013

ORIGIN Germany

ENGINE 1,781 cc, straight-four

TOP SPEED 243 kph (151 mph)

Honda Amaze

The mid-sized Honda Amaze is the saloon version of the hatchback Honda Brio. Although the Amaze shares the same engine as the Brio, its colour options and overall layout, it is set apart by a much larger boot.

YEAR 2013

ORIGIN Japan

ENGINE 1,198 cc, straight-four

TOP SPEED 140 kph (87 mph)

Mercedes-Benz C220 CDI AMG Sport Edition

The C-Class is the second-smallest saloon produced by Mercedes. The AMG Sport Edition has a range of performance features from AMG, the in-house racing engine division of Mercedes-Benz.

YEAR 2014

ORIGIN Germany

ENGINE 2,143 cc, straight-four

TOP SPEED 232 kph (144 mph)

Hatchbacks

A hatchback gets its name from the sloping door at the back of the car's body – called a hatch – that opens upwards. This door is hinged at the top, and it covers a boot, or luggage space, at the rear. Because they are smaller than saloons, hatchbacks are easier to park, which makes them a popular choice for people living in cities.

Fiat Uno

Among small family cars (superminis), the Fiat Uno stands out for its modern seating design, with slightly elevated seats, earning it the nickname "the ultimate supermini". Its aerodynamic design, spacious interior, and fuel efficiency earned it the European Car of the Year award in 1984.

YEAR	1983
ORIGIN	Italy
ENGINE	1,301 cc, straight-four
TOP SPEED	167 kph (104 mph)

The Fiat Uno is the most-produced Fiat car: more than 8,800,000 cars have been built over eight years.

Peugeot 205 GTi

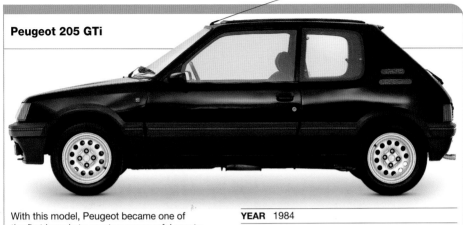

With this model, Peugeot became one of the first brands to create a successful sporty hatchback. Its features include alloy wheels, additional driving lights, and larger bumpers.

YEAR	1984
ORIGIN	France
ENGINE	1,905 cc, straight-four
TOP SPEED	195 kph (121 mph)

Volkswagen New Beetle

This car was inspired by the original "bug-shaped" Volkswagen Beetle. The New Beetle shares many similar features with its ancestor, such as large round rear lights and a rounded roof.

YEAR	1998
ORIGIN	Germany
ENGINE	1,984 cc, straight-four
TOP SPEED	185 kph (115 mph)

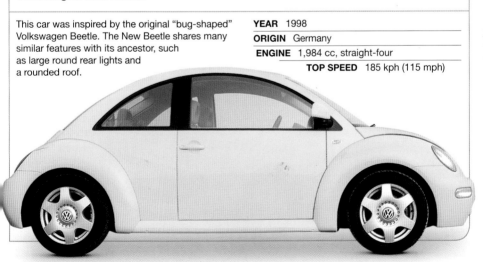

Maruti Suzuki Swift

The Japanese Suzuki Swift was sold in various markets worldwide before being launched in India as the Maruti Suzuki Swift. Its European-style curvy body and sporty performance made it a popular choice among hatchbacks.

Stretched rear light

YEAR 2005

ORIGIN India

ENGINE 1,197 cc, straight-four

TOP SPEED 160 kph (100 mph)

Peugeot 107

This car's small size makes it ideal for city driving, and its carbon dioxide emissions are much lower than most other hatchbacks. However, it has limited boot space and lacks advanced safety systems.

YEAR 2005

ORIGIN France

ENGINE 998 cc, straight-three

TOP SPEED 158 kph (98 mph)

Honda Fit Sport

Unlike the earlier Honda Fit models, the Sport has four different seat options. This allows the owner to increase boot or seating space based on their requirement.

YEAR 2007

ORIGIN Japan

ENGINE
1,497 cc,
straight-four

TOP SPEED
183 kph
(114 mph)

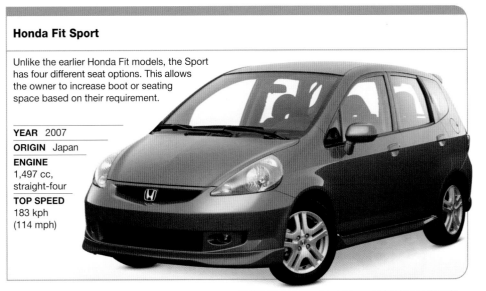

Tata Nano

The world's cheapest new car, the Tata Nano is manufactured by Tata Motors in India. Its design includes cost-saving features. For example, its engine is made of aluminium instead of cast-iron. The engine is positioned in the car's boot, and can only be accessed from inside the car.

YEAR 2009

ORIGIN India

ENGINE 624 cc,
straight-two

TOP SPEED
105 kph (65 mph)

Hyundai i20

With features including six airbags and a braking system that reduces the risk of skidding, the Hyundai i20 has a high safety rating.

YEAR	2008
ORIGIN	South Korea
ENGINE	1,197 cc, straight-four
TOP SPEED	154 kph (95.7 mph)

Headlights can automatically sense darkness

BMW 530d Gran Turismo

The combination of the stylish features of a saloon and the sporty look of a coupé gives this car a unique look. An automatic feature turns the engine off when the car stops, saving fuel.

YEAR	2010
ORIGIN	Germany
ENGINE	2,993 cc, straight-six
TOP SPEED	246 kph (153 mph)

Mercedes-Benz A 250

The first Mercedes-Benz A-Class was produced in 1997. The 2012 edition, Mercedes-Benz A 250, is longer, wider, and lower than most of the earlier models. It has a spacious interior and a big boot.

YEAR   2012

ORIGIN   Germany

ENGINE   1,991 cc

TOP SPEED   240 kph (149 mph)

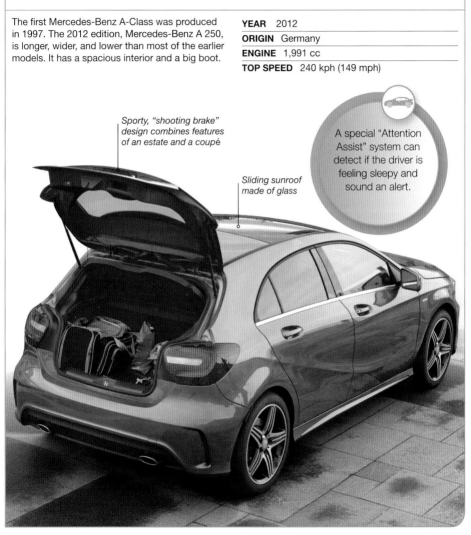

Sporty, "shooting brake" design combines features of an estate and a coupé

Sliding sunroof made of glass

A special "Attention Assist" system can detect if the driver is feeling sleepy and sound an alert.

Convertibles

A convertible car has a movable roof, or top, which means it can be changed from a closed-top to an open-top model. This feature is controlled either manually or automatically.

FOCUS ON...
TOPS
Convertibles have one of two roof types: a hard top or a soft top.

Mazda MX-5

Inspired by the design of British sports cars in the 1960s, the Mazda MX-5 was one of the most successful convertibles of its time. It is famous for its "pop-up" headlights, which lift up from the bonnet when in use.

YEAR	1989
ORIGIN	Japan
ENGINE	1,597 cc, straight-four
TOP SPEED	183 kph (114 mph)

"Pop-up" headlights

Lotus Elise

This stylish, two-seater convertible is recognized by its distinct "bug-eyed" headlights. Its bonded aluminium chassis and fibreglass panels help to reduce both its weight and the cost. At 725 kg (1,600 lb), it weighs half as much as an average saloon.

YEAR	1996
ORIGIN	UK
ENGINE	1,796 cc, straight-four
TOP SPEED	240 kph (150 mph)

▲ A hard top is made out of a rigid material, such as plastic, steel, or aluminium. A car may have a detachable (removable) or a retractable (foldable) hard top.

▲ A soft top is made out of a tough fabric, such as canvas or vinyl. The fabric is mounted on a folding frame.

Aston Martin DB9 Volante

This soft-top Aston Martin comes with a safety feature called "roll-hoops", which protect the occupants if the car were to roll over. These hoops are hidden in the rear headrests and pop out when sensors detect that the car might face an accident.

YEAR	2011
ORIGIN	UK
ENGINE	5,935 cc, V12
TOP SPEED	306 mph (190 kph)

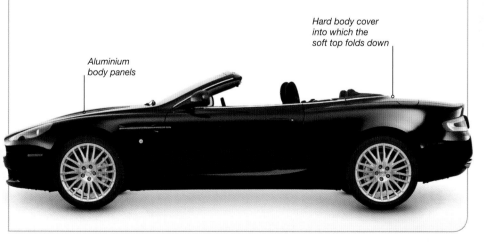

Hard body cover into which the soft top folds down

Aluminium body panels

Infiniti G37 Convertible

The hard top of the Infiniti G37 is made up of three hinged panels. When the top goes down, these panels fold into the boot, leaving little space for anything else.

YEAR 2009

ORIGIN Japan

ENGINE 3,696 cc, V6

TOP SPEED 250 kph (155 mph)

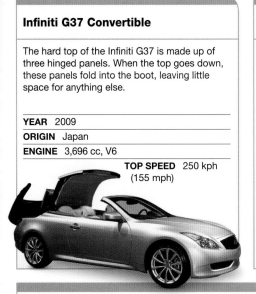

Volkswagen Golf Cabriolet MK6

The design of this convertible is based on the hatchback version of the Volkswagen Golf. Its folding fabric top can open in only 9.5 seconds, even when the car is driven at a speed of 30 kph (19 mph).

YEAR 2011

ORIGIN Germany

ENGINE 2,480 cc, straight-five

TOP SPEED 209 kph (130 mph)

Porsche 911 Carrera S Cabriolet

The Porsche 911 Carrera S Cabriolet has an electronic screen, called a "wind-deflector", which pops up behind the rear seats. It cuts down wind and noise levels in the car when the top is down.

YEAR 2012

ORIGIN Germany

ENGINE 3,800 cc, flat-six

TOP SPEED 301 kph (187 mph)

Electrically operated, folding fabric roof

Chevrolet Corvette Stingray Convertible C7

This convertible has an aluminium frame that makes it 45 kg (100 lb) lighter than previous, steel-framed models. The soft top also reduces weight.

YEAR	2014
ORIGIN	USA
ENGINE	6,200 cc, V8
TOP SPEED	290 kph (180 mph)

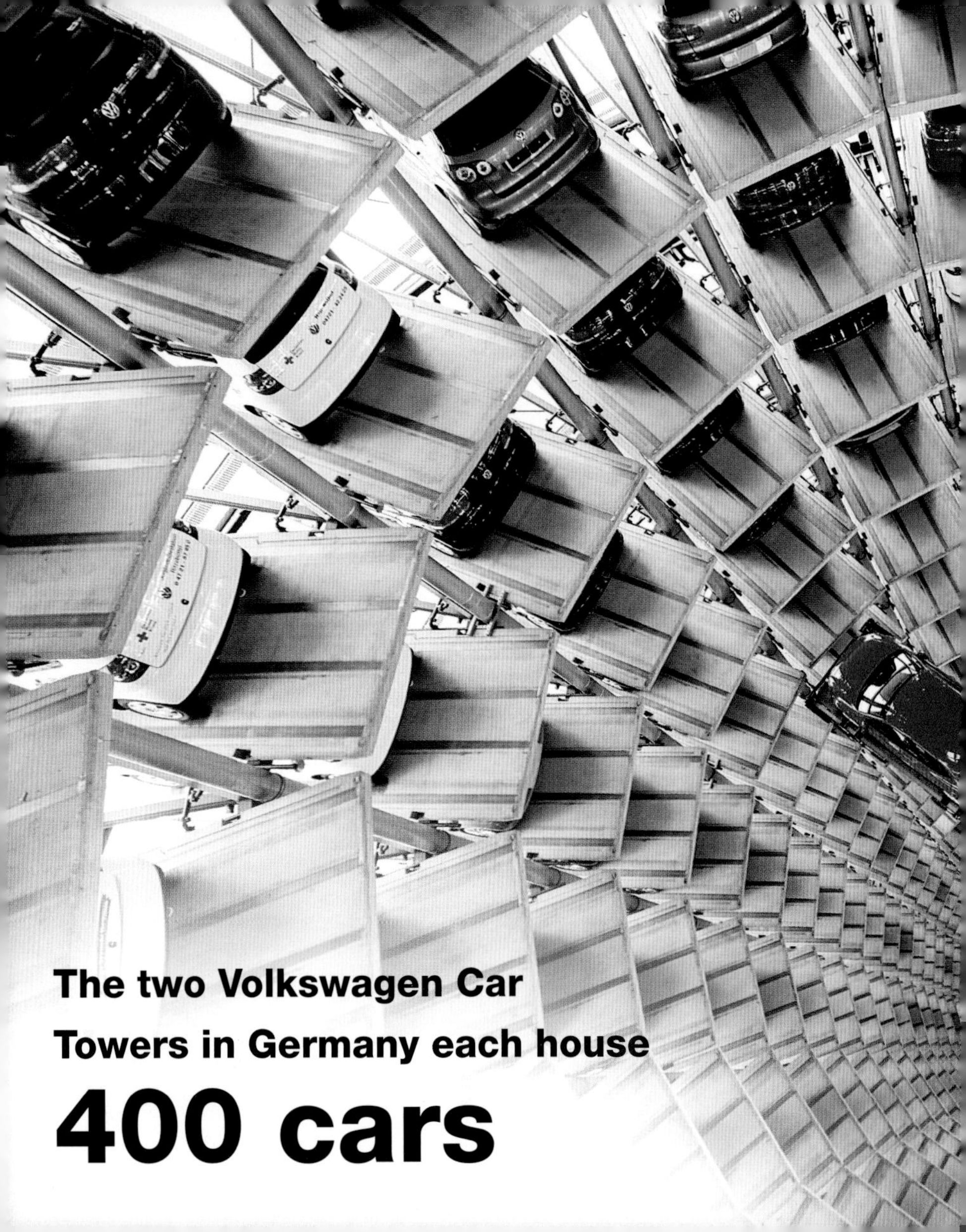

The two Volkswagen Car
Towers in Germany each house
400 cars

CAR TOWERS
The cars produced at the world's largest car factory – Autostadt, in Germany – are stored in the two 20-storey-high Volkswagen Car Towers. The cars from the factory are delivered on a conveyor belt and moved around inside the tower by a lift. Cars can travel up and down the tower at a speed of 7 kph (4.5 mph).

Coupés

In the 19th century, coupés were horse-drawn carriages with a seat for two people. Today, the word "coupé" refers to a car with at least two seats, and, typically, two doors and a fixed, sloping roof. Some also come in hatchback and four-door versions.

Audi TTS

Light and fast, the Audi TTS comes with a magnetic suspension system, which adapts to uneven road surfaces for a smoother ride.

YEAR	2008
ORIGIN	Hungary
ENGINE	1,984 cc, straight-four
TOP SPEED	250 kph (155 mph)

Rolls-Royce Phantom Coupé

The aluminium body of the Phantom Coupé is lightweight but strong. The car shares many features with its saloon version, such as a luxurious interior and powerful engine. Its doors are hinged at the rear rather than front. The navigation cameras give a 360-degree view of the surroundings, making parking and reversing easier.

YEAR	2008
ORIGIN	UK
ENGINE	6,752 cc, V12
TOP SPEED	250 kph (155 mph)

Bentley Continental GT Speed

The front grille of the Bentley Continental GT Speed has been designed to improve engine cooling. The smaller-than-usual steering wheel makes it easy to manoeuvre the car.

YEAR 2007

ORIGIN UK

ENGINE
5,998 cc, W12

TOP SPEED
325 kph (202 mph)

The design of the boot lid in estate cars varies. It can be hinged at the top, side, or bottom.

▲ In a split-gate boot lid, the rear window swings upwards and the lower lid downwards.

▲ As the name suggests, a side-hinge boot lid has a single door that is hinged on the side.

▲ A dual-hinge boot lid has a pair of doors that are hinged on each side, and open outwards.

Estates

An estate car, or station wagon, is a type of saloon with a roof that extends to the rear. Unlike a saloon, it does not have a separate boot. Instead, there is a space behind the rows of seats where luggage can be kept, which can be accessed through a rear door.

Mercedes-Benz E-Class W124

The Mercedes-Benz E-Class W124 has an aerodynamic design that reduces fuel consumption. It has only one windscreen wiper, but it can reach to most of the windscreen.

The W124 is a well-made car that typically lasts for up to 500,000 km (300,000 miles).

YEAR	1985
ORIGIN	Germany
ENGINE	4,192 cc, V8
TOP SPEED	250 kph (155 mph)

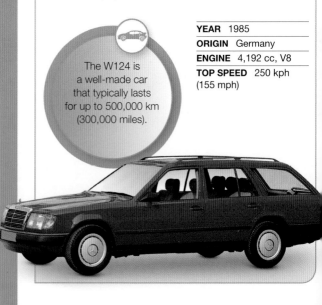

Jaguar X-type Sportwagon

Hooded, oval headlights

The first estate created by Jaguar, this car is based on the X-type saloon. However, the rear doors and body structure are completely redesigned. To avoid the typical "boxy" look of an estate, the roof is made to slope down towards the rear.

YEAR	2004
ORIGIN	UK
ENGINE	2,967 cc, V6
TOP SPEED	196 kph (122 mph)

Ford Mondeo Mk IV

The windscreen of the fourth generation Ford Mondeo is designed to keep out the Sun's heat. Its front grille vent opens when the car is being driven, to keep the engine cool. Once the car picks up speed, the vent closes.

YEAR	2007
ORIGIN	Germany
ENGINE	2,261 cc, straight-four
TOP SPEED	195 kph (121 mph)

BMW Mini Clubman

The BMW Mini Clubman has a dual-hinge boot lid and an extra "club door" on the driver's side, which is hinged from the rear. The club door can be opened after the front door to make it easier to get to the rear seats.

YEAR 2008

ORIGIN UK

ENGINE 1,598 cc, four-cylinder

TOP SPEED 201 kph (125 mph)

Ford Focus ST Wagon

This estate's unique Sport Steering System helps the driver to turn by increasing the sensitivity of the steering wheel. This feature is also useful when parking in tight spaces.

YEAR 2012

ORIGIN Germany

ENGINE 2,500 cc, straight-five

TOP SPEED 248 kph (154 mph)

Mercedes-Benz CLS Shooting Brake

The spacious Shooting Brake was the second car in the world, after the Mercedes CLS, to have LED headlights, which use less energy and are brighter than standard bulbs.

Audi A6 Avant

The 2011 Audi A6 Avant consumes 18 per cent less fuel than the previous model of the car. This is because its chassis is made mainly of aluminium, which makes it lighter in weight.

YEAR	2011
ORIGIN	Germany
ENGINE	2,995 cc, V6
TOP SPEED	250 kph (155 mph)

YEAR	2012
ORIGIN	Germany
ENGINE	4,633 cc, V8
TOP SPEED	250 kph (155 mph)

Hyundai i30 Wagon

The Hyundai i30 Wagon has a spacious interior and can carry more luggage than the model's hatchback version. It even has an underfloor compartment for extra storage space.

YEAR	2013
ORIGIN	South Korea
ENGINE	1,591 cc, straight-four
TOP SPEED	192 kph (119 mph)

People carriers

Also known as multi-purpose vehicles (MPVs), people carriers are tall, spacious cars that can carry five to eight passengers. Like the front row, the middle and back rows are often made up of individual seats, which can be folded or removed.

Mitsubishi Space Wagon

This was one of the first MPVs. It came in five- and seven-seat versions. It was sold under different names, including the Chariot, the Nimbus, and the Expo.

YEAR	1984
ORIGIN	Japan
ENGINE	1,725 cc, straight-four
TOP SPEED	156 kph (97 mph)

Ford Windstar

The Windstar was Ford's first MPV with front-wheel drive (where the engine's power goes to the front wheels only). Smoother performance and handling gave it an edge over other MPVs of its time.

YEAR	1994
ORIGIN	USA
ENGINE	3,797 cc, V6
TOP SPEED	187 kph (116 mph)

Volkswagen Sharan

This car gets its name from a Persian word meaning "Carrier of kings". Around 670,000 Sharan cars were made over 15 years.

YEAR	1995
ORIGIN	Portugal
ENGINE	2,792 cc, V6
TOP SPEED	177 kph (110 mph)

Renault Kangoo 1

The rear seats of the adaptable Renault Kangoo can be removed to make more room. Because it is a tall car, it can be used if an occupant needs to fit in a wheelchair.

YEAR	1997
ORIGIN	France
ENGINE	1,390 cc, straight-four
TOP SPEED	156 kph (97 mph)

Mercedes-Benz Viano

The people carrier version of the Mercedes-Benz Vito van – the Viano – has a stylish interior, most models being fitted with storage cabinets and a folding table. It is a spacious car that comes in three different body lengths.

YEAR 2004

ORIGIN Spain

ENGINE 2,143 cc, straight-four

TOP SPEED 188 kph (117 mph)

A variant called Marco Polo has a wardrobe, a rear seat that can be turned into a bed, and a pop-up roof for more headroom.

Indicator lights mounted on wing mirrors

Volkswagen Touran

The 2006 Volkswagen Touran is an improved
version of the 2003 model. One of the most
interesting additions is that of ParkAssist
technology, which parks the car automatically,
without the driver holding the steering wheel.
The ParkAssist gauges the speed
and available space, and avoids
surrounding objects.

YEAR	2006
ORIGIN	Germany
ENGINE	1,984 cc, straight-four
TOP SPEED	200 kph (124 mph)

Peugeot 5008

Peugeot's first medium-sized people carrier, the 5008
is one of the more spacious, yet stylish, cars of the type.
The middle seats can be folded down all the way
to the floor, providing more luggage space.
Top-of-the-range models have a glass roof
that extends all the way to the rear.

YEAR	2009
ORIGIN	France
ENGINE	1,598 cc, straight-four
TOP SPEED	195 kph (121 mph)

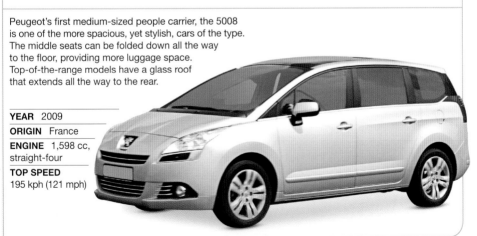

Chevrolet Orlando

Originally introduced as a concept car in 2008, the Chevrolet Orlando is relatively compact for a seven-seater. It has three rows of tiered seating, which allows a clear view for passengers on the back seats as they sit slightly higher than those in the front.

YEAR	2010
ORIGIN	USA
ENGINE	2,384 cc, straight-four
TOP SPEED	200 kph (124 mph)

Citroën C4 Picasso

The C4 Picasso draws on features of Citroën's recent concept cars, with LED running lights in the front and a rounded nose. Its unusual windscreen creates a sense of space, and improves visibility for the driver.

Wide-angle windscreen

YEAR 2013

ORIGIN France

ENGINE 1,598 cc straight-four

TOP SPEED 187 kph (116 mph)

Toyota Prius V

With the Prius V, Toyota has expanded its range of Prius hybrid (powered by petrol and electricity) models to four. This one has a larger body than the other Prius models, and also features a unique roof, made of a lightweight resin, which is 40 per cent lighter than a glass roof of the same size.

YEAR 2011

ORIGIN Japan

ENGINE 1,798 cc straight-four

TOP SPEED 166 kph (103 mph)

One of the Mini Coopers used in the 2003 film *The Italian Job* had

two steering wheels

AN UNUSUAL FEATURE
Many films feature car stunts, including car-chase scenes and car jumping stunts. For one such scene in *The Italian Job* (2003), a Mini Cooper was custom-built with two steering wheels. This helped the actors to perform while a stuntman actually drove the car.

SUVs

A sport utility vehicle (SUV) is designed to cope with driving on rough terrain. Most SUVs have four-wheel drive, in which the engine powers all four wheels instead of only the front or the rear wheels. The first SUVs were based on military vehicles.

FOCUS ON...
SIZE
SUVs can be divided into three broad groups, based on their size: mini, compact, and full-size.

Lexus GX J120

The GX J120 was Lexus's third SUV. The exterior of this eight-seater was inspired by the Toyota Land Cruiser Prado, with both cars sharing similar dimensions.

YEAR	2003
ORIGIN	Japan
ENGINE	4,664 cc, V8
TOP SPEED	197 kph (122 mph)

▲ A mini SUV, such as the Nissan Juke, is usually less than 4.2 m (13.7 ft) long.

▲ A compact SUV, such as the Toyota RAV4, is typically 4.25–4.6 m (14–15 ft) long.

▲ A full-size SUV, such as the Mercedes-Benz GL Class, is usually at least 5 m (17 ft) long.

Hummer H2

The H2 was the second vehicle in the Hummer range. Just as the H1 before it, its design was based on the US military vehicle, the Humvee. The Hummer H2 has the frame of a light truck and is wider than typical city cars.

YEAR	2003
ORIGIN	USA
ENGINE	5,967 cc, V8
TOP SPEED	176 kph (109 mph)

Nissan Armada

Built on the same body framework as Nissan's pickup truck Titan, the Armada is a full-size SUV. It can seat up to eight people.

YEAR 2004

ORIGIN Japan

ENGINE
5,552 cc, V8

TOP SPEED
193 kph
(120 mph)

Mercedes-Benz GL Class

The seven-seater GL boasts a number of luxury features, such as heated rear seats. Larger than comparable cars, it has a higher roof and a huge boot space with a capacity of 200 litres (53 gallons).

YEAR 2006

ORIGIN Germany

ENGINE 2,987 cc, V6

TOP SPEED
199 kph (124 mph)

Jeep Patriot

One of the cheapest SUVs available in its size, this compact SUV retains all of the features of a typical Jeep, including round headlights, vertical windows, and a wide radiator grille.

YEAR 2007

ORIGIN USA

ENGINE 1,968 cc, straight-four

TOP SPEED 188 kph (117 mph)

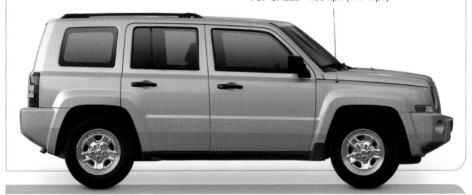

Chevrolet Tahoe

The Tahoe was revised in 2007 with a new bonnet and grille, new door panels, and new seat designs. It can seat nine people, but the third row of seats cannot fold flat. This gives it limited boot space.

YEAR 2007

ORIGIN USA

ENGINE 5,300 cc, V8

TOP SPEED 180 kph (112 mph)

Audi Q5

Audi's first compact SUV has an innovative roof rack with sensors that allow the car to automatically adjust its centre of gravity when the rack is loaded, helping the car to stay balanced.

YEAR	2009
ORIGIN	Germany
ENGINE	2,967 cc, V6
TOP SPEED	225 kph (140 mph)

Ford Escape Hybrid

The Ford Escape was the first hybrid SUV, launched in 2004. It was given a face-lift in 2009, with added features, such as improved interior lighting and heated front seats.

YEAR	2009
ORIGIN	USA
ENGINE	2,488 cc, straight-four
TOP SPEED	164 kph (102 mph)

BMW X5 xDrive50i

The xDrive is a powerful car with a new turbocharged diesel and petrol engine. The headlights and fog lights sit high and close to the radiator grille, giving it a rugged appearance. Some optional features include a Lane Departure Warning, which identifies the car's movement away from marked lanes with the help of side-mounted cameras. The steering wheel starts vibrating to alert the driver in such situations.

YEAR 2011

ORIGIN Germany

ENGINE 4,395 cc, V8

TOP SPEED 210 kph (131 mph)

Luxury cars

Luxury cars are owned as status symbols, commanding steep price tags and possessing extravagant features. Often, just a few cars of a particular model are produced, making them even more exclusive. Sometimes made-to-order, these cars promise high levels of passenger comfort, customized interiors, and an enhanced driving experience.

TRAVELLING IN STYLE
Most luxury car brands provide the option of personalized accessories, such as luggage, which are often customized to match the car's interior.

Luxury cars

Luxury (top-end) cars are sleek, very expensive, high-performance machines. These exclusive vehicles are bought by wealthy people as a sign of social status. Such cars are decorated using the finest materials and come with optional extravagant features.

Interior style

The interior of a luxury car can be fitted with plush seats, made with the finest leather and fabrics, in the buyer's favourite colours. The ceiling can even be lined with crystals, as here.

Choosing the best

The privileged buyers of these fashionable cars can choose different trims, materials, colours, and expensive fittings. Some luxury cars are completely hand-built – all parts, exterior and interior, are put together manually.

Personalization

Apart from choosing from trims available from the car manufacturer, buyers can add personal touches to their vehicles. Some may opt for placing their initials or signature on the seats or car exterior, while others have their car's dashboard styled with inlays of wood from their trees.

Wheels

There are different types of upmarket wheel designs available. Wheels could be coated with gold or studded with diamonds.

ACCESSORIES

Expensive accessories are standard in luxury cars, and are often personalized.

"Infotainment systems", include touchscreen or voice controls, Wi-Fi connectivity, surround-sound streamed music, and mobile charging points.

Minibar and glass holders can be fitted in the car for keeping refreshments handy.

Limousines

Usually longer than a standard car, a limousine is often associated with wealth because of its luxurious appearance. A typical limousine has a separate compartment for the driver, and is driven by a chauffeur. This expensive car is often hired for special events, such as weddings and parties.

Hummer H2 Limousine

This eight-wheeled Hummer H2 stretch limousine (longer than typical limousines) can carry up to 16 passengers. Like other limousines, it can be fitted with lights and music systems.

Volvo S80 Limousine

Based on the S80 saloon, the S80 limousine was developed by Volvo in collaboration with Nilsson Karosserifabrik. It is available in four- or six-door variants. A five-door version of the S80 is also used as a hearse.

YEAR 2002
ORIGIN Sweden
ENGINE 2,922 cc, straight-six

YEAR 2003

ORIGIN USA

ENGINE 6,200 cc, V8

Range Rover Limousine

The stretched version of a popular SUV, the Range Rover limousine has been designed for luxury. It comes with a "jet door" – a door that opens upwards like the door of a small jet plane.

YEAR 2002

ORIGIN UK

ENGINE 4,999 cc, V8

Jet door

The US presidential limousine has its own oxygen supply

Grand tourers

A grand tourer, or GT, is a stylish car that can be driven over long distances. It is capable of high speed, but, unlike a sports car, it has a luxurious interior built for comfort. The name refers to an 18th-century tradition of grand tours, where young people from wealthy families took a cultural tour across Europe.

Jaguar XJS V12

The sleek XJS has a padded top. With a popular two-door, full convertible style and a V12 engine, this model became one of the most successful grand tourers of its time.

YEAR	1988
ORIGIN	UK
ENGINE	5,343 cc, V12
TOP SPEED	241 kph (150 mph)

Ford Mustang GT

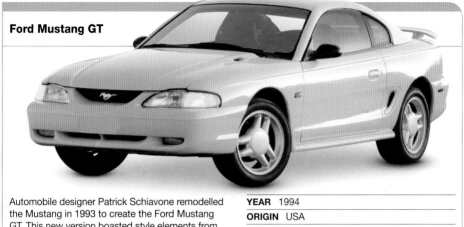

Automobile designer Patrick Schiavone remodelled the Mustang in 1993 to create the Ford Mustang GT. This new version boasted style elements from earlier models, and a high-performance V8 engine. It earned the title 1994 Motor Trend Car of the Year.

YEAR	1994
ORIGIN	USA
ENGINE	4,942 cc, V8
TOP SPEED	219 kph (136 mph)

Porsche 911 Carrera Cabriolet

In 1998, Porsche's 911 sports car received its most significant upgrade since its launch in 1963. The latest model featured a new water-cooled engine.

YEAR	1998
ORIGIN	Germany
ENGINE	3,600 cc, flat-six
TOP SPEED	274 kph (170 mph)

Curved headlight

Ferrari Enzo

Sleek side panels add to aerodynamic design

Ferrari's Enzo is named after the company's founder, Enzo Ferrari. This car is inspired by cutting-edge Formula 1 design and technology. Its compact size, reduced weight, revolutionary cabin design, and a gear shifting time of 150 milliseconds makes it the ultimate sports car for the road.

YEAR 2002

ORIGIN Italy

ENGINE 5,998 cc, V12

TOP SPEED 363 kph (226 mph)

Pontiac GTO

The Pontiac GTO can accelerate from 0 to 97 kph (60 mph) in about 5 seconds. The addition of bright wheel spokes and a spoiler adds a sporty edge to its appearance.

YEAR 2006

ORIGIN Australia

ENGINE 6,375 cc, V8

TOP SPEED 282 kph (175 mph)

Audi R8

The two-seater R8 uses Audi's trademark Quattro four-wheel drive system. It has an aluminium, lightweight chassis, and has a more spacious interior than other sports cars. Its superior technology and smooth ride makes it a true rival to the iconic Porsche 911.

YEAR 2006

ORIGIN Germany

ENGINE 5,204 cc, V10

TOP SPEED 315 kph (196 mph)

Nissan GT-R SpecV

A special variant of the Nissan GT-R, the GT-R SpecV is 60 kg (132 lb) lighter than the standard version. This car features some carbon-fibre body panels, no rear seats, and a titanium exhaust – a lightweight alternative to a steel one.

YEAR	2007
ORIGIN	Japan
ENGINE	3,799 cc, V6
TOP SPEED	311 kph (193 mph)

Dodge Challenger

The long-bonnet design of the Challenger is a tribute to the compact, powerful American cars of the 1970s. However, its performance matches that of modern-day cars. While it offers a smooth ride and handles well, many feel the interior does not match up to the dramatic exterior.

YEAR 2008

ORIGIN USA

ENGINE 6,059 cc, V8

TOP SPEED 233 kph (145 mph)

Mercedes-Benz SLS AMG

This model was the first Mercedes-Benz car to be designed in-house by its development wing – AMG. The most iconic feature of the two-door grand tourer is its "gull-wing" doors, which open upwards.

Gull-wing doors

YEAR 2010

ORIGIN Germany

ENGINE 6,208 cc, V8

TOP SPEED 317 kph (197 mph)

Chevrolet Camaro 2SS

The Camaro 2SS is known for its sleek exterior and powerful performance. Its short side window, small, high-mounted tail light, and low roofline with sloping windscreen add to the appeal.

YEAR	2010
ORIGIN	USA
ENGINE	6,162 cc, V8
TOP SPEED	250 kph (155 mph)

Racing and sports cars

From long-distance rallies to high-speed track-based competitions, car racing has been popular since cars first appeared. While sports cars are powerful enough to be raced occasionally if the owner wants to, racing cars are set apart by their speed and design, and are raced by highly skilled drivers.

RACING TYRES
Different tyres are used for different conditions: intermediate tread tyres for wet tracks; heavy tread tyres for standing water; and slick tyres for dry tracks.

The world of racing

The first car races were organized in the 1890s, to prove the speed and reliability of the vehicles involved. Soon, it became a popular source of entertainment, and different categories of races were introduced. Today, motor racing is an international sport.

Stock car racing

Stock car races are typically held on an oval track. NASCAR (National Association for Stock Car Racing) is the largest body that organizes these races. The Sprint Cup Series is the most popular NASCAR race in the USA.

Rallying

In rally races, cars run between two controlled stops (special stages) on public or private roads, instead of a track. Pairs of drivers aim to arrive first or match a stipulated time.

Drag racing

Drag racers compete in pairs on a short, standard track – usually 400 m (1,320 ft) in length. The first to cross the finishing line wins.

Formula racing

Formula racing gets its name from early motor racing championships, held in Europe. These had set rules, or a "formula", that every participant had to follow. Today, formula racing includes Formula One, Two, and Three series.

Speedsters

Both racing and sports cars are built for speed, but only sports cars appear in showrooms for sale to the public. Racing cars may be closed-wheel (with wings covering the wheel) or open-wheel (without wings). They are modified for competing in various championships.

Racing cars

High-performance racing cars are designed specifically to take part in various types of motor racing. Modifications include adding more engines, lowering the car's height, and removing the wings.

Stock car
Stock cars resemble ordinary street models but their chassis, tyres, and accessories are modified for speed and safety. These cars compete in racing events such as NASCAR.

Go-kart
A small, open-wheeled car built for racing, a go-kart can reach speeds of up to 250 kph (155 mph). Some go-karts are fitted with a specially designed engine.

Formula car
Formula cars have a long bonnet, single seat, and open cockpit. The engine is placed behind the driver.

Air flow

Aerodynamics is the study of the flow of air around a moving object, such as a car. Cars are designed with features that fight drag (air resistance) to improve speed and reduce lift, which could flip a car.

Rear spoiler, or wing, stabilizes car at high speeds by reducing drag

Rounded front wing channels airflow over the car

Low, flat underbody allows smoother airflow beneath the car

Front spoiler, or air dam, decreases amount of air passing underneath the car

Front air inlet can be closed to lessen drag

Sports cars

Equipped with strong engines and designed to be sleek and lightweight, sports cars are usually production vehicles (made for sale) that provide the thrill of driving at high speeds.

Roadster
Agile, two-seater roadsters, such as this BMW Z4, are usually open-top cars. They may come with a soft top or a retractable hard top.

Supercar
Costly supercars are exceptional, superfast sports cars, featuring state-of-the-art racing technology.

Racing cars

Built for speed and agility, racing cars are usually one- or two-seater vehicles designed to be driven in racing competitions. Cars for different types of race, such as Formula or drag racing, have specifically modified engines and body shapes.

FOCUS ON...
F1 FLAGS

In an F1 race, different flags are used to indicate the condition of the track or to relay important messages to the drivers.

▲ A red flag signals that the race has been stopped for safety reasons and that all drivers must pull in.

▲ A striped flag warns drivers of substances on the track, including water, oil, and debris.

▲ The chequered flag is shown to declare the winner and to signal that the race is officially over.

Ferrari F138

Designed for the 2013 Formula One (F1) Season, the lightweight F138 was driven by the two-time World Champion Fernando Alonso. The name – F138 – is a combination of the race year and the number of engine cylinders. The car has a high nose, while the rear is narrow, which makes it more aerodynamic.

YEAR	2013
ORIGIN	Italy
RACE	F1

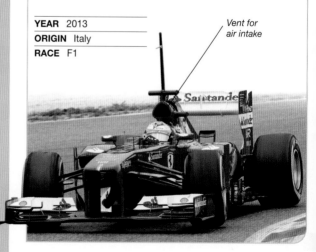

Vent for air intake

McLaren Mercedes MP4-28

Launched on 31 January 2013 as part of McLaren's 50th anniversary celebration, the MP4-28 has a completely new design – with a new chassis and a higher nose. However, it failed to perform well in the races.

YEAR	2013
ORIGIN	UK
RACE	F1

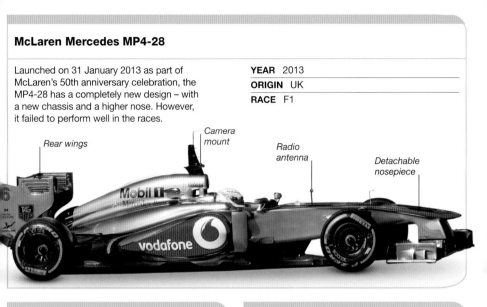

Rear wings

Camera mount

Radio antenna

Detachable nosepiece

Red Bull Racing RB9

The RB9 was driven by Sebastian Vettel, the three-time winner of the World Driver's Championship, which is awarded to the F1 driver of the season. This car faced the disadvantage of being fitted with tyres that wore out more quickly during a race than other cars' tyres.

YEAR	2013
ORIGIN	UK
RACE	F1

Mercedes AMG Petronas F1W05

The F1W05 has a smooth, wide nose, unlike the typical raised nose of a Formula car. The downturned nose makes the car more aerodynamic.

YEAR	2014
ORIGIN	Germany
RACE	F1

Camera mount on the nose

Habermann Top Methanol Dragster

This dragster (car used in drag racing) was driven by Dennis Habermann, who was third in the 2012 FIA European Drag Racing Championship. Although similar in design to Top Fuel dragsters, Top Methanols are less powerful. They are powered by fuel that is 100 per cent methanol, while Top Fuel dragsters use a fuel mixture that is only 10 per cent methanol.

Top Methanol Dragsters can cover 0.4 km (0.25 miles) in less than 6 seconds, reaching speeds of up to 400 kph (248 mph).

YEAR 2012

ORIGIN Germany

RACE Top Methanol

Castrol GTX High Mileage Ford Mustang

The High Mileage Ford Mustang was driven by 16-time Funny Car race champion, John Force. Funny Car dragsters look similar to production cars but have custom-built chassis. Ford Mustangs have been used in drag racing since 1964.

YEAR 2009

ORIGIN USA

RACE Funny Car

Cylinder

Mountain View Tire Dodge Avenger

Driven by the youngest-ever winner of the National Hot Rod Association (NHRA) Pro Stock class, Vincent Nobile, the Dodge Avenger has been modified as per NHRA's strict regulations. Nobile reached a top speed of 339.61 kph (211.03 mph) with the Dodge Avenger.

YEAR	2012
ORIGIN	USA
RACE	Pro Stock

SEAT Léon

The Léon was first introduced to the World Touring Car Championship in 2005. SEAT won the manufacturer's title in 2008 and 2009 with this car. A limited edition road-going model, the Cupra World Champion Edition, was built in 2010 to celebrate the successful race season.

YEAR 2009

ORIGIN Spain

RACE World Touring Car Championship

Ford Fusion

When a NASCAR car is taking a sharp turn at high speed, the air flowing underneath it can lift it off the ground. The Ford Fusion has a low and wide front bumper, which blocks this air flow, making it safer to drive.

YEAR 2011

ORIGIN USA

RACE NASCAR

Chevrolet Impala

Richard Childress Racing Team's Chevrolet Impala was driven by Kevin Harvick up until the 2013 season. Harvick won the race at the 2012 Phoenix International Raceway and finished third overall in the 2013 Sprint Cup Series.

YEAR	2012
ORIGIN	USA
RACE	NASCAR

Honda Civic

Pirtek Racing team's Honda Civic participates in the British Touring Car Championship, a race event for saloons. It is fitted with a low-cost, turbocharged engine, which matches the specifications required for all touring racing cars.

YEAR	2013
ORIGIN	UK
RACE	British Touring Car Championship

Superkart 250 cc

The fastest go-kart in the world, a Superkart 250 cc can complete laps faster than more technologically advanced racing cars. It can reach a top speed of 257 kph (160 mph), and is primarily used in the British Superkart Championship.

YEAR	Unknown
ORIGIN	Unknown
RACE	British Superkart Championship

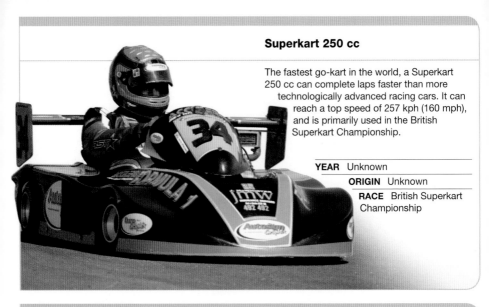

Subaru Impreza WRC

Introduced in 1993, the Impreza WRC has performed well in rally races over the years. The 2004 model had improved aerodynamics, a turbocharged engine, and four-wheel drive (where the engine's power goes to the front and rear wheels).

YEAR	2004
ORIGIN	Japan
RACE	World Rally Racing

Swamp Thing

The Swamp Thing is a monster truck, which is a modified pickup truck with giant wheels. This vehicle weighs a hefty 5,000 kg (11,000 lb). Apart from competing in monster truck races, it also participates in entertainment events, such as crushing smaller cars and performing stunts.

YEAR 2004

ORIGIN UK

RACE Monster truck racing

Ferrari's fastest ever
pit stop took only

1.95 seconds

PIT STOP
A racing car makes a pit stop in order to get new tyres and have minor repairs between laps. Pit stops are in a lane that runs parallel to the racing track. The team's pit crew must complete all the tasks as fast as possible for the car to get back in the race. An average F1 pit stop lasts about 2.5 seconds.

Roadsters

Traditionally, a roadster was defined as a car with no windows and, sometimes, no doors. Nowadays, however, a roadster is any two-seater convertible, open-top car (without a fixed roof). This sporty car has a lightweight structure, and can have a soft top or a hard top.

BMW Z1

The Z1 was BMW's first open two-seater since the late 1950s. A unique feature of this car is that its doors can be retracted vertically down into the car's body. The body itself is high enough to offer protection even when the doors are down.

YEAR	1989
ORIGIN	Germany
ENGINE	2,494 cc, six-cylinder
TOP SPEED	225 kph (140 mph)

All BMW Z1s were left-hand drive, except the final one, which was also the only Z1 to be hand-built.

Marcos Mantula Spyder

The Spyder is the convertible variant of the 1984 Marcos Mantula coupé. Technologically, the two cars are similar, except that the Spyder has a stiffer chassis to make up for the open roof. It also has a rounded nose and a padded soft top.

YEAR	1986
ORIGIN	UK
ENGINE	3,532 cc, V8
TOP SPEED	224 kph (139 mph)

Alfa Romeo Spider

The Alfa Romeo Spider has a typical Italian design, with a low body that is broad and flattened. It is fitted with the trademark Alfa Romeo grille, round headlights, and has a steeply sloping windscreen. Although it has a high rear, the boot space is small.

YEAR	1995
ORIGIN	Italy
ENGINE	2,959 cc, V6
TOP SPEED	225 kph (140 mph)

Renault Sport Spider

Built to promote Renault as a sporting brand, the Sport Spider is a lightweight car with an aluminium chassis and a plastic body. It has neither a roof nor a top and only Sport Spiders sold in the UK have a windscreen.

YEAR	1996
ORIGIN	France
ENGINE	1,998 cc, straight-four
TOP SPEED	211 kph (131 mph)

Honda S2000 AP1

First shown as a concept car in 1995, the S2000 AP1 was launched in 1999. This stylish car is equipped with a vinyl soft top. An aluminium hard top is available as an optional extra.

YEAR	1999
ORIGIN	Japan
ENGINE	1,997 cc, straight-four
TOP SPEED	241 kph (150 mph)

Lamborghini Murcièlago Roadster

Fighter aircraft, Spanish architecture, and mega-yachts were among the things that inspired the styling of this impressive, soft-top Lamborghini. The Murcièlago has a low-tech, manually operated roof.

YEAR 2004
ORIGIN Italy
ENGINE 6,496 cc, V12
TOP SPEED 322 kph (200 mph)

Audi TT RS Roadster

The TT RS is equipped with an engine designed exclusively for it, and no other Audi car used it until the RS3 in 2011. This powerful engine, combined with the lightweight aluminium chassis and body, provides a smooth ride.

YEAR 2009
ORIGIN Germany
ENGINE 2,479 cc, straight-five
TOP SPEED 250 kph (155 mph)

Supercars

Supercars are very expensive sports cars. They are usually produced in limited numbers, which makes them exclusive and highly prized. Equipped with the latest technology, these powerful performers are capable of reaching extremely high speeds.

Ferrari 288 GTO

Originally built for racing, the 288 GTO did not end up on the track, as the race category it was designed for was discontinued. This limited edition car was released only in Ferrari's iconic red colour.

YEAR	1984
ORIGIN	Italy
ENGINE	2,855 cc, V8
TOP SPEED	306 kph (190 mph)

Aston Martin V8 Zagato

Recognized for its unique angular design, the V8 Zagato is one of the rarest supercars. Aston Martin decided to make only 52 cars of this model, and all of them were bought before its production, solely on the basis of drawings and a scale model.

YEAR	1986
ORIGIN	UK
ENGINE	5,340 cc, V8
TOP SPEED	300 kph (186 mph)

McLaren F1

In its time, the McLaren F1 succeeded in breaking multiple speed records. It can reach such high speeds that its engine compartment has to be lined with gold foil, to shield against the heat produced.

YEAR 1992

ORIGIN UK

ENGINE
6,064 cc, V12

TOP SPEED
391 kph
(243 mph)

Lamborghini Diablo VT Roadster

With this car, Lamborghini continued its tradition of naming its models after fighting bulls. The Diablo VT Roadster was a convertible version of the coupé. It earned its supercar status as it was one of the fastest cars of its time.

YEAR 1995

ORIGIN Italy

ENGINE 5,707 cc, V12

TOP SPEED
323 kph (201 mph)

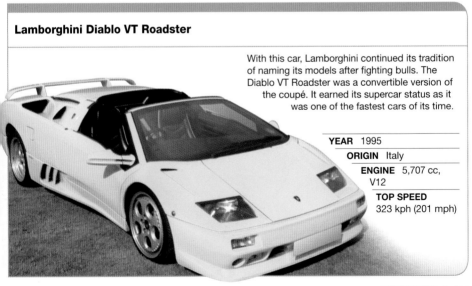

Alfa Romeo 8C Competizione

This car's design was inspired by the Alfa Romeo models of the 1950s and 1960s. Its name is a tribute to Alfa Romeo's racing tradition: "8C" is a reference to the eight-cylinder engine used by most Alfa Romeo race cars in the 1930s, and "Competizione" is Italian for "competition".

YEAR 2007

ORIGIN Italy

ENGINE 4,591 cc, V8

TOP SPEED
292 kph (181 mph)

Lamborghini Aventador LP 700-4

Parts of this sleek two-seater's body, including the roof and doors, are made of carbon fibre. While this makes the car body extremely strong, the use of aluminium in other parts makes the Aventador light as well.

YEAR 2011

ORIGIN Italy

ENGINE 6,498 cc, V12

TOP SPEED 350 kph (217 mph)

Bugatti Veyron 16.4 Grand Sport

One of the fastest and most expensive convertibles in the world, this supercar has two removable roofs. One of them is a manually removable hard top, made of transparent polycarbonate. The other is a soft top that unfolds over the cabin, much like a flat umbrella.

YEAR	2009
ORIGIN	France
ENGINE	7,993 cc, W16
TOP SPEED	407 kph (253 mph)

The Bugatti Veyron
Super Sport was the world's

fastest road car

for three years, with a

top speed of 431 kph (267.8 mph)

Amazing cars

Some cars are set apart by their unusual designs or extremely powerful engines, while others look to change the concept of what a car is or how it can be run. Record breakers, usually jet-propelled, show how fast a car can go, while amphibious cars make it possible to drive cars through water. Several cars are built purely as concepts to show off advanced technologies and designs.

ELECTRIC CARS
Some cars – such as this Venturi Fétish, the world's first two-seater electric sports car – run only on electricity, using energy stored in batteries.

Out of the ordinary

In the history of car design and technology, a few special vehicles mark significant breakthroughs. These cars led the way with innovations in speed, fuel efficiency, safety, styling, or mechanics. Some vehicles are even designed for use in outer space!

Eco cars

Environmentally friendly cars are built from sustainable materials where possible and produce low or zero emissions. This all-electric BMW i3 is powered by a rechargeable battery.

Speed demons

Supersonic cars, such as the Bloodhound SSC, are designed to travel faster than the speed of sound. Powered by both a jet and a rocket engine, this car is in development to shatter the world land speed record by achieving a speed just over 1,600 kph (1000 mph).

On land and water

Versatile and fun, amphibious vehicles, such as the WaterCar Panther, can cruise motorways, climb sand dunes, or jet along a river faster than a motor cruiser.

Concept cars

Prototype cars showcase new strategies in design and technology. Previewed in 2011, this state-of-the-art hybrid Ford Evos featured many new design concepts, such as front and rear gull-wing doors.

Front gull-wing door

LED strip headlights

CARS IN SPACE

Space cars, or rovers, are built for space exploration. NASA's *Curiosity*, shown here, is controlled from Earth, and conducts scientific experiments on Mars, collecting rock samples and photographing the terrain.

Hybrid cars

Cars that use more than one power source – usually a combination of a petrol engine and an electric motor – are called hybrid cars. These vehicles are more fuel efficient and emit (give out) lower levels of air pollutants.

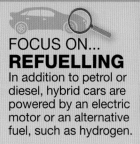

FOCUS ON...
REFUELLING

In addition to petrol or diesel, hybrid cars are powered by an electric motor or an alternative fuel, such as hydrogen.

Honda Insight

The Honda Insight is fitted with an electric motor that boosts the performance of its petrol engine. In addition to the hybrid drive system, its lightweight body and streamlined design also help to improve the car's fuel efficiency.

YEAR	2000
ORIGIN	Japan
ENGINE	995 cc, straight-three
TOP SPEED	170 kph (106 mph)

Most of the body is made up of aluminium and plastic

Saturn Vue Green Line

The first hybrid SUV created by General Motors, the Saturn Vue Green Line is a mild hybrid. This means that the electric motor is used to assist the main engine but cannot be used independently. This model uses up to 20 per cent less fuel than a regular Saturn Vue.

YEAR	2007
ORIGIN	USA
ENGINE	2,376 cc, straight-four
TOP SPEED	160 kph (99 mph)

◄ Charging points can be used to recharge the batteries of an electric hybrid car.

◄ Although not as common as charging points, hydrogen filling stations have been opened in many countries.

Toyota Prius

The 1997 Toyota Prius was the first hybrid car to be mass-produced. The 2004 Prius is a full hybrid, which means that power from the petrol engine and the electric motor can be shared to run the car.

YEAR	2004
ORIGIN	Japan
ENGINE	1,497 cc, four-cylinder
TOP SPEED	170 kph (106 mph)

Toyota Highlander

The mid-sized SUV Highlander is a full hybrid, known for its smooth ride and spacious interior. However, it is more expensive than other SUV hybrids, and not particularly fuel efficient in comparison to other cars of the same type.

YEAR 2007

ORIGIN Japan

ENGINE 3,310 cc, straight-six

TOP SPEED 180 kph (112 mph)

Chevrolet Volt

Introduced as a concept vehicle in 2007, the Volt is a full hybrid, plug-in electric car. The electric battery is powerful enough for city driving. The Volt also has a gas-powered engine, which can be used for longer distances.

YEAR 2011

ORIGIN USA

ENGINE 1,398 cc, straight-four

TOP SPEED 161 kph (100 mph)

LaFerrari

The LaFerrari's design is inspired by the brand's racing cars. Only 499 units of this sports car are planned. Unlike most hybrid vehicles, the internal combustion engine and the electric motor of the LaFerrari can run at the same time.

Nissan Cima

The luxury saloon Cima combines powerful engine performance with elegant design and a spacious interior. Its efficient hybrid technology significantly reduces the harmful emissions produced.

YEAR 2012

ORIGIN Japan

ENGINE 3,498 cc, V6

TOP SPEED 150 kph (93 mph)

YEAR 2013

ORIGIN Italy

ENGINE 6,262 cc, V12

TOP SPEED 350 kph (218 mph)

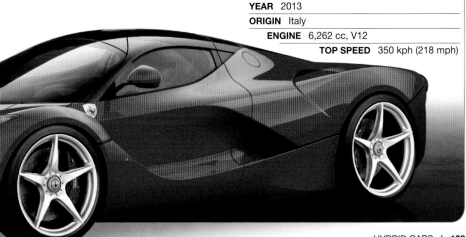

Record breakers

The first land speed record – the highest speed by a vehicle on land – was set in 1898 by Count Gaston de Chasseloup-Laubat, who drove 1 km (0.62 miles) in 57 seconds, in an electric motor-powered vehicle. Modern-day record breakers use rocket or jet engines.

Blue Flame

Driven by American racing car driver Gary Gabelich, the rocket-powered Blue Flame achieved a world land speed record on the Bonneville Salt Flats in Utah, USA, on 23 October 1970. This record remained unbroken until October 1983.

YEAR	1970
ORIGIN	USA
SPEED	1,015 kph (630.4 mph)
LENGTH	11.4 m (37.4 ft)

Thrust2

After Thrust1 crashed in 1977, its driver Richard Noble improved the design and went on to build, and pilot, Thrust2. On 4 October 1983, Thrust2 broke Blue Flame's world land speed record. It was powered by a single Rolls-Royce Avon turbojet engine.

YEAR	1983
ORIGIN	UK
SPEED	1,019.4 kph (633.5 mph)
LENGTH	8.3 m (27.2 ft)

Body design is strong and rigid to withstand high speeds

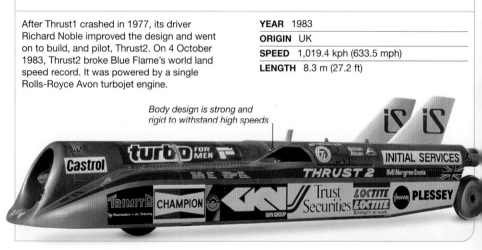

ThrustSSC

ThrustSSC was the first supersonic car – one designed
to be faster than the speed of sound. On 15 October 1997,
it became the first car to officially break the sound barrier,
and currently holds the world land speed record.

ThrustSSC's
two engines
burn 18 litres
(4.75 gallons) of
fuel per second.

YEAR	1997
ORIGIN	UK
SPEED	1,227.98 kph (763.04 mph)
LENGTH	16.5 m (54 ft)

Bloodhound SSC

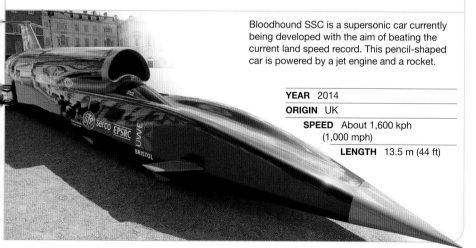

Bloodhound SSC is a supersonic car currently
being developed with the aim of beating the
current land speed record. This pencil-shaped
car is powered by a jet engine and a rocket.

YEAR	2014
ORIGIN	UK
SPEED	About 1,600 kph (1,000 mph)
LENGTH	13.5 m (44 ft)

Amphibious cars

Amphibious cars can travel both on land and on or even under water. Most land vehicles can be adapted for driving on water by fitting them with a waterproof body. Some use propellers to move forwards, while others use high-powered water jets.

▲ Amphibious buses are used for city sight-seeing trips, carrying tourists on both roads and rivers.

▲ Amphibious boats can be used for tourism in places where there is a need to cross both land and water.

▲ Armoured amphibious military tanks are used for defence and patrol work.

Amphicar Model 770

The Amphicar was the first amphibious car to be mass produced. A pair of propellers were mounted under the rear bumper to push it through water. This car steered with its front wheels not just on land, but even in water.

YEAR	1961
ORIGIN	Germany
ENGINE	1,147 cc, straight-four
TOP SPEED	Land: 110 kph (70 mph); Water: 11 kph (7 mph)

In 1965, four Englishmen crossed the English Channel in two Amphicars in just seven hours.

Gibbs Aquada

Once the Gibbs Aquada enters the water, its wheels retract, its road lights change to water lights, and a powerful jet is started to push it through the water. The entire process takes only four seconds. This three-seater car has no doors, which helps to prevent leaks.

YEAR 2003

ORIGIN New Zealand

ENGINE 2,500 cc, V6

TOP SPEED Land: 161 kph (100 mph);
Water: 56 kph (35 mph)

WaterCar Python

In 2010, the WaterCar Python became the fastest amphibious vehicle in the world. However, it never went into production. Watercar has now built the Panther, an amphibious SUV with specifications similar to that of the Python.

YEAR 2009

ORIGIN USA

ENGINE 2,997 cc, V6

TOP SPEED Land: 201 kph (125 mph);
Water: 97 kph (60 mph)

Cars in space

Scientists have developed special machines that have been driven on the surface of the Moon and Mars. Most of these vehicles, called rovers, are operated remotely from Earth, and send back scientific data for scientists to study.

Lunokhod 1

This was one of two rovers built and sent to the Moon by the Soviet Union (a group of states that included modern-day Russia). It was controlled by radio signals from Earth and returned more than 20,000 images from the Moon in just 10 months.

SIZE	1.35 m (4.5 ft) tall
WEIGHT	756 kg (1,665 lb)
LAUNCH DATE	10 November 1970

Lunar Roving Vehicle

The first rover to be driven on the Moon (rather than being controlled remotely) was a battery-powered vehicle that could carry two astronauts and their equipment. It travelled at a top speed of 18.5 kph (11.5 mph). Three such rovers were built, one for each of the last three missions to the Moon.

SIZE	3 m (10 ft) long
WEIGHT	210 kg (465 lb)
LAUNCH DATE	First launched with *Apollo 15* on 26 July 1971

Sojourner

The first rover to be operated on another planet, *Sojourner* was powered by solar panels arranged on its top and could travel at the speed of 1 cm (0.4 in) per second. It sent back information about the chemical make-up of the rocks on Mars, and the wind and weather conditions there.

SIZE   65 cm (25.5 in) long

WEIGHT   10.6 kg (23 lb)

LAUNCH DATE   4 December 1996

Wind sensors on top of antenna

The rover was named after Sojourner Truth, a woman who travelled across North America to fight for women's rights.

Solar panels

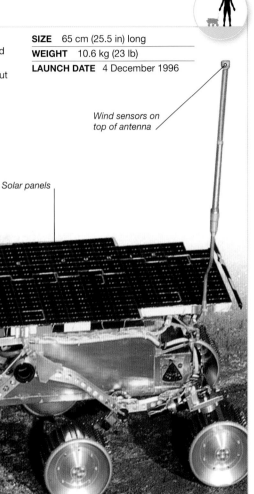

Opportunity

In 2003, NASA sent two identical
rovers – *Opportunity* and *Spirit* – to Mars with
the aim of collecting and studying the Martian
soil for signs of life. Both rovers could travel at
a maximum speed of 50 mm (2 in) per second.
Communication from *Spirit* ended in 2010, but
Opportunity continues to send back data.

SIZE	1.6 m (5.3 ft) long
WEIGHT	174 kg (385 lb)
LAUNCH DATE	7 July 2003

*Camera on top of
mast can rotate
360 degrees*

*Gold-painted body
helps to maintain
temperature*

The spacecraft that
carried *Curiosity* to
Mars took 253 days to
cover the 566 million km
(352 million miles)
between Earth
and Mars.

Curiosity

This six-wheeled rover is about the same size as a small SUV. It carries equipment that can collect and analyze rock and soil samples. *Curiosity* is designed to drive over obstacles up to 65 cm (25 in) high and can travel about 200 m (660 ft) every day. It has a top speed of 4 cm (1.5 in) per second.

SIZE	3 m (10 ft) long
WEIGHT	900 kg (1,985 lb)
LAUNCH DATE	26 November 2011

Antenna

Strong outer body protects computer and electronic systems

Each wheel can move independently, making it easy to steer the rover over rough surfaces

A fully charged battery can power a solar car for up to
400 km
(250 miles)

Some modern cars are powered by solar energy (energy from the Sun). These cars are covered in solar panels, which absorb and convert the Sun's energy into electricity. Some solar cars, such as the Solarworld No.1 (shown here) are built to take part in races.

Concept cars

A car created to feature an unusual new design or exciting technology is called a concept car. Concept cars are usually shown at major car shows to test new ideas and attract attention. They are one-of-a-kind models that may or may not be built for sale.

Volvo YCC

Special paint does not allow dirt to cling on easily

Gull-wing door

The YCC (Your Concept Car) is the first concept car to be designed by an all-female team. The front is lower and the rear slants back more than a typical Volvo, allowing the driver to see all four corners of the car. Other features include run-flat tyres that last for a safe distance even after a puncture.

YEAR	2004
ORIGIN	Sweden
TOP SPEED	Not stated

Mercedes-Benz F700

This large saloon is powered by a new DiesOtto engine, which combines the fuel efficiency of a diesel engine with the low emissions of a petrol engine. The vehicle has two laser scanners to detect uneven surfaces, allowing the car to adjust for a smoother ride.

YEAR 2008

ORIGIN
Germany

TOP SPEED
200 kph
(124 mph)

Mercedes-Benz F-Cell Roadster

Inspired by the 1886 Mercedes-Benz Motorwagen, this concept car's design resembles that of a horseless carriage. This hydrogen-electric hybrid produces no harmful emissions. Other features include a joystick instead of a steering wheel, and big spoked wheels with thin, solid rubber rims.

YEAR 2009

ORIGIN Germany

TOP SPEED
25 kph (15 mph)

Cadillac Urban Luxury Concept

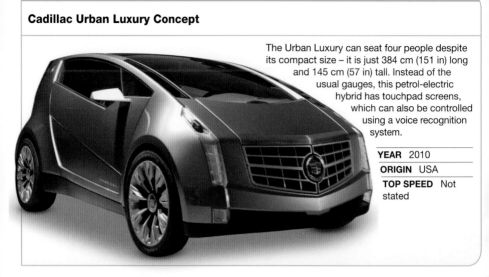

The Urban Luxury can seat four people despite its compact size – it is just 384 cm (151 in) long and 145 cm (57 in) tall. Instead of the usual gauges, this petrol-electric hybrid has touchpad screens, which can also be controlled using a voice recognition system.

YEAR	2010
ORIGIN	USA
TOP SPEED	Not stated

Volvo Air Motion Concept

Designed to weigh less than 454 kg (1,000 lb), this car has a simple design with fewer and lighter body parts than other cars. Instead of an internal combustion engine, it is powered by compressed air motors, which further reduces the weight.

YEAR	2010
ORIGIN	Sweden
TOP SPEED	Not stated

Mercedes-Benz Biome

With the help of special hybrid technology, the Biome releases oxygen instead of carbon dioxide. The car's body is made of a material called BioFibre, which is grown in a laboratory.

YEAR	2010
ORIGIN	Germany
TOP SPEED	Not stated

Jaguar C-X75

This two-seater supercar has four electric motors, each turning one wheel. The electric motors are powered by a gas turbine instead of a conventional piston engine. In 2011, Jaguar announced production of the C-X75 in collaboration with the Williams F1 racing team. However, production was cancelled in 2012.

YEAR 2010

ORIGIN UK

TOP SPEED 330 kph (205 mph)

Aluminium body, with a carbon-fibre chassis

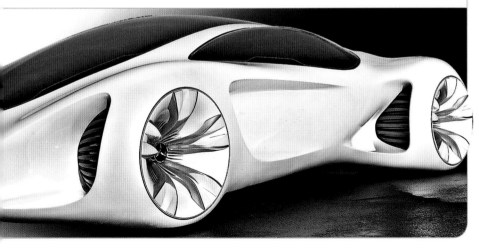

BMW i8 Concept

The futuristic BMW i8 is powered by a petrol engine and an electric motor. The interior of this eco-friendly car is made up mainly of recycled material. Instead of LED headlights, it uses new laser technology that is a thousand times more powerful.

Butterfly doors open up and out

YEAR 2011
ORIGIN Germany
TOP SPEED
250 kph (155 mph)

Jaguar C-X16

This is the smallest Jaguar since 1954. Its petrol engine and electric motor can be used independently or together. A button on the steering wheel allows the driver to boost the engine's performance with the electric motor.

YEAR 2011
ORIGIN UK
TOP SPEED 300 kph (186 mph)

Audi Urban Concept

This ultra-light two-seater concept car has a carbon fibre body, weighing just under 500 kg (1,100 lb). The driver can adjust the steering wheel and pedals to his own body measurements in this narrow car. Despite the size, the Urban Concept also has a small, drawer-like luggage compartment.

YEAR 2011

ORIGIN Germany

TOP SPEED 100 kph (62 mph)

Protective mudguards on wheels, which stand away from chassis

Driver's seat is placed 30 cm (12 in) ahead of the passenger's seat to give more elbow and shoulder room

Toyota Fun-Vii Concept

This car's exterior and interior colour and design can be changed to suit the driver's mood. The Fun-Vii also has a pop-up avatar projected from the dashboard to help the driver understand the car's futuristic features. The car seats three people.

LED-screen exterior can be used as a display, with changing wallpapers

YEAR 2011

ORIGIN
Japan

TOP SPEED
Not stated

Lexus LF-LC

The Lexus Future-Luxury Coupé features an enormous front grille and day-running headlights – each shaped like an "L". The car is also equipped with a racing car-inspired steering wheel, and touchscreens for controlling the windows and adjusting the seats.

YEAR 2012

ORIGIN Japan

TOP SPEED Not stated

Audi Sport Quattro Concept

Designed to celebrate the 30th anniversary of the first Audi Sport Quattro model, this sporty concept car's body is mostly made up of carbon fibre, while the doors are aluminium.

YEAR 2013

ORIGIN Germany

TOP SPEED 305 kph (190 mph)

Toyota i-Road

The three-wheeled, electric-powered i-Road can seat two people, one behind the other. It has a meter that calculates how much the driver is leaning when taking a turn, and limits the angle of the turn. This ensures the car never tips over. The steering wheel vibrates to let the driver know when the car is tilting at its maximum angle.

YEAR 2013

ORIGIN Japan

TOP SPEED 60 kph (37 mph)

Fun cars

Some cars are truly unique, with very unusual designs. While many of these cars are modified for fun, or specially built by companies for promoting their goods, a few are based on the designer's own ideas about what a car is and what it could do.

Dusty Dave the Dolphin

Dusty Dave is an adapted 1972 Volkswagen Beetle. Its exterior was modified by sculptor Tom Kennedy so that it looked like a dolphin. Its mouth is hinged to open.

YEAR	1996
ORIGIN	USA
DESIGNED BY	Penny Smith and Harry Leverette

Ford 1932 Hot Rod

This Ford 1932 Model B has been redesigned more recently as a hot rod car, with its bonnet removed to show off the engine. A hot rod is fitted with a modified, powerful engine, and is often painted in bright colours that add to its appeal.

YEAR	1932
ORIGIN	USA
DESIGNED BY	Unknown

Wienermobile

Shaped like a hot dog on a bun, the Wienermobile is used by the Oscar Mayer Company to advertise its products. The first Wienermobile was built in 1936, and six tour the USA today. This 2004 model has gull-wing doors, a hot dog-shaped dashboard, and mustard- and ketchup-coloured seats. The drivers of these cars are called "hotdoggers".

YEAR	2004
ORIGIN	USA
DESIGNED BY	Prototype Source

Wenzhou shoe car

Built by a shoe company to promote its brand, this shoe-shaped electric car is made of the same leather the company uses for its footwear. It took six months to construct this car, which is 3 m (10 ft) long and 1 m (3.3 ft) high.

YEAR	2011
ORIGIN	China
DESIGNED BY	Kang Shoe Company

Wind-powered car

This wind-powered car runs on two sets of generators and batteries that are connected to a fan in the front. As the car moves, the fan spins, producing electricity for the vehicle. Solar panels at the back also help generate electricity.

YEAR	2012
ORIGIN	China
DESIGNED BY	Tang Zhenping

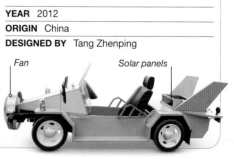

Fan *Solar panels*

The Rinspeed sQuba is the first car that not only runs on roads, but can also travel under water